A2 Ethics

Revision Guide for Edexcel (Unit 3)

Peter Baron & Laura Mears

Published by Inducit Learning Ltd trading as pushmepress.com,

Mid Somerset House, Southover, Wells,

Somerset BA5 1UH, United Kingdom

www.pushmepress.com

First published in 2011, second edition 2012

ISBN: 978-1-909618-55-8

Contents

4

How to Get an A Grade

Effective learning involves reducing difficult topics into smaller, "bite-sized" chunks.

Every revision guide, card or study guide from PushMe Press comes with its own website consisting of summaries, handouts, games, model essays, revision notes and more. Each website community is supported by the best teachers in the country.

At the end of each chapter you will see an `i-pu-sh` web link that you can type into your web browser along with a QR code that can be scanned by our free App.

These links will give you immediate access to the additional resources you need to "Get an A Grade" by providing you with the relevant information needed.

Getting an A Grade has never been easier.

Download our FREE How to Get an A Grade in Ethics App for your phone or tablet and get up-to-date information that accompanies this book and the whole PushMe Press range.

http://ethics.pushmepress.com/download

Introduction to Ethics

At AS level we considered the interaction between religion and morality, as well as two major **TELEOLOGICAL** theories, which put the focus on consequences. We then looked at how these apply to the issue of War and Peace and Sexual Ethics.

At A2 level we continue to go deeper into the connections between religion and morality and we now turn our focus to **DEONTOLOGICAL** theories, which all claim that there are some **ABSOLUTES** in morality. We then apply this to the issues of **JUSTICE, LAW** and **PUNISHMENT**. The additional area here is the whole subject of **META-ETHICS**, the study of meaning in statements about ethical rights and wrongs.

KEY TERMS

- **CONSCIENCE** - May come from **GOD**, our **UPBRINGING** or a process of **REASON**. "Where does conscience come from and how does it operate?" **PSYCHOLOGY** merges with philosophy here.

- **DETERMINISTS** - See every event, including human choice, as having an antecedent **CAUSE**. The question arises: "Where does this leave moral **RESPONSIBILITY** and free will?"

- **INSTRUMENTAL THEORIES OF VALUE** - See goodness relative to some end, such as human happiness. But in the debates within ethics, what do **DEONTOLOGISTS** like Kant or **TELEOLOGISTS** like Joseph Fletcher or JS Mill have to say about sexual ethics?

- **INTRINSIC THEORIES OF VALUE** - See something as good-in-itself. Does the environment have intrinsic value? Which part of it?

- **META-ETHICS** - Concerns the nature and meaning of the words good and right. A key question in meta-ethics is: "Is goodness **OBJECTIVE** (linked to moral facts in the world) or **SUBJECTIVE** (up to me)?"

- **VIRTUE ETHICS** - Studies virtues and vices as **CHARACTER** traits or **HABITS**. Virtue ethics asks: "What character traits do I need to practise to build the excellent life?"

THE ETHICS TOOLKIT

The study of ethical theories at AS and A2 has equipped us with a toolkit which we can use to assess any ethical issue. In this toolkit we derive insights from different theories.

KANT has given us the **PRINCIPLE OF UNIVERSALISABILITY**, a method of reasoning implying **CONSISTENCY** and a neutral point of view, and **PERSONAL AUTONOMY**, that places human choice and reason as a central ethical concern.

AQUINAS has given us the **PRINCIPLE OF NATURAL RATIONAL PURPOSE:** the idea of an order of being which is appropriate to our unique rational natures. The ultimate **TELOS** is **EUDAIMONIA** - well-being or personal and social flourishing.

UTILITARIANS have given us the **LEAST HARM PRINCIPLE**: the idea that we should always assess consequences in the light of an empirical calculation of the balance of happiness over misery, pleasure over pain or **WELFARE** over harm. In Economics we talk of **COST/BENEFIT** analysis.

RELATIVISTS encourage us to consider the **PRINCIPLE OF CULTURAL DIVERSITY** and to be humble in the face of claims that our own culture is objectively superior. All theories are to some extent children of their times.

It is important to note that our theories overlap to some extent and may not be as opposed as we sometimes think. For example, all of them discuss and claim for themselves the **GOLDEN RULE** "Do to others as you would have them do to you," Matthew 7:18 (is this therefore a good example of a universal ethical absolute?).

All appeal to **VIRTUE** or character traits (**MILL** appeals to sympathy,

KANT to dutifulness, **FLETCHER** to love, **AQUINAS** to practical wisdom and the Christian virtues of 1 Corinthians 13, faith, hope and love).

All theories have a **TELEOLOGICAL** aspect. Kant, for example, considers consequences in so far as he asks us to universalise the consequences of everyone doing what I do. He also envisages a goal, the **SUMMUM BONUM** which is similar in some ways to Aristotle's **EUDAIMONIA**. Moreover, Aquinas' **NATURAL LAW** is best described as "a deontological theory arising out of a Greek teleological worldview" where the good is defined by the rational ends (**TELOS**).

And our third deontological theory - **DIVINE COMMAND** whilst revering the rules of God, also sees the ultimate end to be like Christ, fulfilling our true humanity which is perfected in him, in the afterlife and also (crucially) the present age which is a society called the **KINGDOM OF GOD** - one family where love and justice are supreme.

Interestingly, RM **HARE** who we meet in the **META-ETHICS** section with his theory of **PRESCRIPTIVISM** is a Kantian preference utilitarian (and former tutor of Peter Singer). He is a Kantian in his theory of how moral language works, and yet a preference utilitarian in how we make right choices. The utilitarian philosopher **HENRY SIDGWICK** was also greatly influenced by Kant.

Critiques of the Relationship Between Religion and Morality

At AS we examined the merits or otherwise of Divine Command Theory, and we introduced the Euthyphro Dilemma. It is best to read this section in the AS study guide first, and then use the material here to build on these debates. The specification is very open-minded about which debates you consider. It is better to go into depth of evaluation on two or three approaches, with mature evaluation, rather than rapidly firing through them all.

MORAL ARGUMENTS FOR THE EXISTENCE OF GOD

The Fourth of **AQUINAS'** Five Ways, the moral argument sets forth grounds for belief in God on the basis that the existence of morality necessitates the existence of God. **KANT'S CATEGORICAL IMPERATIVE** is actually a starting point here, because it suggests that there are certain obligations that we are duty-bound to fulfil, such as keeping our promises. As a **UNIVERSAL ABSOLUTE**, it is binding on everyone that this duty should be observed, and hence we have the basis for moral objectivity or **NORMATIVITY**. It is now simply a case of asking, where do these norms come from? A swift application of **OCKHAM**'s razor will take us to the simplest conclusion: God.

Critique

The argument rests on an assumption; that there is a universal standard of morality. Many relativists would question this, arguing that all morality is based on environmental or cultural factors. JL Mackie argues that values emerge out of **FORMS OF LIFE.** These are beliefs, habits, and patterns of behaviour which determine what is approved as "right" and what is approved as "wrong."

James Rachels' Argument

In response, James **RACHELS** argues that **MACKIE** makes a logical error here, because when he says "there are no **OBJECTIVE** truths," this is itself an **ABSOLUTE** statement. A **RELATIVIST** ends up with an **ABSOLUTE** conclusion. How can we possibly know? Secondly, we need to look at the **EVIDENCE** for objective values. When Colin **TURNBULL** studied the IK tribe in Kenya, he noticed values such as cruelty to the elderly, extreme selfishness in food distribution, scorn for the weak - but also the tribe was **DISINTEGRATING**. So, if we don't share some common **OBJECTIVE** values eg respect for life, compassion, co-operation the human race will not **FLOURISH**. We have established an objective test for goodness. We can also ask, why is it that some principles like the **GOLDEN RULE** "do as you would be done by" can be found in all ethical systems and religions? Go to the Golden Rule website for a full list. Admittedly this is a **NATURALISTIC** argument some would reject - that goodness can be observed in some **NATURAL FEATURE** of the world, or humanity, such as Richard **DAWKINS** who argues for an genetically programmed, evolved "**LUST** to be **NICE**" or altruistic gene.

A PSYCHOLGICAL CHALLENGE

This challenge draws on material from the A2 Philosophy of Religion revision guide (Non-existence of God and critiques of belief). It is fine to have some overlap, provided you keep the material relevant to the interaction between religion and morality.

Many psychologists would look for the causes of religious phenomena in the interactions of the human mind, rather than in some objective spiritual reality.

Sigmund Freud (1856-1939)

FREUD believed that at the heart of the psychological need for religion was **GUILT**. This drew on a popular anthropological idea of the time, known as the **PRIMAL HORDE**. At some point in our ancestry, the young men in the tribe, frustrated by the control of the women exerted by the dominant male, rise up and kill their father. Afterwards, they feel guilt, which feeds their need to reinstate the father figure. For Freud, religion is a **PROJECTION OF UNCONSCIOUS NEEDS** in the id (unconscious self). We need a father figure; one isn't to hand, so we employ a substitute in the Father God. These needs are then reinforced through the super-ego, which insists on rituals and behaviours which keep our primitive, unconscious desires in check. Hence our standards of morality come not from an external moral law-giver, but from the guilt within, and the environment without.

Critique of Freud

Freud's view has drawn largely on Darwinistic evolution, which carries a great deal of weight. It has also been influenced by respected thinkers

13

such as Rousseau and Hume, who believed that religion was a distortion of human reason. Hans **KÜNG** criticises Freud's theory for being a **CIRCULAR ARGUMENT**. Drawing on Feuerbach's ideas, he begins from the assumption that religion is a projection, so it is not surprising that he arrives at the conclusion that religion is wish-fulfilment. **KÜNG** also makes the point that although one's religious views can be heavily influenced by their relationship with their earthly father, this does not mean that God is purely a projection, for example in the case where religious believers seem to have excellent relationships with their fathers. Although Freud sees his approach as scientific, (in contrast to the Christian approach), it rests on ideas, rather than proof.

THE EUTHYPRO DILEMMA REVISTED

This is the way the dilemma is often put: Does God command what is good because it is good or is it good because God has commanded it?

- If God commands what is good because it is good, then God adheres to a standard of goodness outside of himself. This would mean that there is something above God, which would question whether he is God, and goodness would be the new supreme standard. Yet many Christian philosophers would see this as a mis-representation of the relationship between God and goodness. If God is good, then part of his essence is goodness, it is not a separate thing outside of himself. This may seem illogical to the human mind, but the argument takes similar form to the theological problems associated with the Trinity, or the Incarnation: it is beyond our minds to perceive of a unity of two things we see as separate and distinct. To see them this way, may be to commit the error of **ANTHROPOMORPHISM**, where we ascribe human characteristics to God.

- If x is good because God has commanded it, then God could command anything at random, and it would be good, with standards of goodness changing at the whim of the almighty. Yet the character of God may help us to solve this dilemma: God as an omnipotent, omniscient and omni-benevolent creator is not capricious; he will not command random acts of immorality, calling them good. Christians like John Lennox, a prolific thinker who debates with Richard Dawkins, says he finds the acts of genocide commanded by God in the Old Testament as the biggest challenge to his faith. Yet even here, can the appeal to God's sovereignty, his abhorrence of the worship of foreign gods, and the understanding that this world is God's, help us understand why God wants his people to be holy? Some evangelicals claim that a bigger question may be: "Why does God put up with any of us selfish sinners on his earth?"

So one of three positions must be taken; morality derives from religion, morality derives from somewhere other than religion, or the more extreme position, religion is adverse to morality. This is a position taken by **RICHARD DAWKINS**, who chooses many examples where religious people hold extreme views, to show how religion, far from doing good, does evil. In his Channel 4 programme The Root of all Evil? Dawkins quotes Stephen Weinberg: "Without religion you have good people doing good things, and evil people doing evil things. But for good people to do evil things, it takes religion"(Quoted in Tyler and Reid, A2 Religious Studies). Yet it may be interesting to consider whether the word "evil" holds any content if there is no absolute standard of right and wrong. Furthermore, Dawkins fails to consider or account for the many atrocities committed by atheist societies, in places such as the Gulags in Communist North Korea today.

GET MORE HELP

Get more help with religion & mortality by using the links below:

http://i-pu.sh/D1N16S23

Kantian Deontology

A **NORMATIVE** theory (tells you what is right and wrong/what you ought to do), that is **DEONTOLOGICAL** (acts are intrinsically right and wrong in themselves, stressing rules and duties), **ABSOLUTIST** (applies universally in all times, places, situations) and is **A PRIORI** (derived from reason alone, not experience).

AUTONOMY

The key Kantian assumption is that we are **AUTONOMOUS** moral agents (self-ruled) with free choice and free reason, rather than **HETERONOMOUS** meaning "ruled by others," where the others could be God, your peer group, or the Church. Kant adopted the **ENLIGHTENMENT** slogan "dare to reason" and was awakened out of his slumbers by reading Jean-Jacques **ROUSSEAU'S** theory of the social contract.

GOOD WILL

Kant argues that the only thing that is morally good without exception is the **GOOD WILL**. A person of good will is someone motivated by **DUTY** alone. They are not motivated by self-interest, happiness or a feeling of sympathy. The good will is an **INTRINSIC** good (it is good in itself and not as a means to something else) and it doesn't matter if it doesn't bring about good consequences. Even if the good will achieved nothing good - even if it were combined with all manner of other evils - "it would shine forth like a jewel, having full value in itself." He contrasts this with other qualities (such as courage) which **CAN** be good but might also be bad depending on the situation (eg a courageous suicide bomber) which are **EXTRINSIC** goods as they depend on the circumstances.

DUTY

Kant argues that we must follow our duty. It is not about what we want to do (our **INCLINATIONS**) or what will lead to the best consequences: only the action which springs from duty is a moral action. Doing your duty (for example, helping a beggar) may be pleasurable, but this cannot be the reason why you did your duty (the **MOTIVE**). For it to be moral you have to act because it is your duty, and **FOR NO OTHER REASON**.

CATEGORICAL IMPERATIVE (CI)

How do you know what your duty is? Kant argues that this comes from the **CATEGORICAL IMPERATIVE**. It is categorical because it applies to us universally - simply because we have rational wills. By contrast a **HYPOTHETICAL IMPERATIVE** takes the form "If you want X, then you must do Y" (for example, if you want to lose weight, then you must stop eating so much). The difference is the categorical imperative applies to us unconditionally, without any reference to a goal we might have (it is simply the form "You must do Y").

CI 1 - The Formula of Law

> "So act that the maxim of your action may be willed as a universal law for all humanity."

For any action to be moral, you must be able to **CONSISTENTLY UNIVERSALISE** it. For example, if you decide not to keep a promise, then you must be able to consistently imagine a world where **EVERYONE** doesn't keep their promises - something Kant thought was impossible (because then no-one would believe a promise and so promise-keeping would vanish). He calls this a **CONTRADICTION IN NATURE** because the very nature of the thing - promising - is destroyed and so the action becomes self-contradictory.

CI 2 - The Formula of Ends

> "Never treat people simply as a means to an end but always also as an end in themselves."

People are **RATIONAL** and **AUTONOMOUS** (self-legislators) and so are worthy of respect. We cannot ONLY use them as a means for getting something else, but always as rational beings with dignity. We universalise our common humanity - which means we treat others as equals, with rights.

CI 3 - The Formula of Autonomy

Kant imagines a community of purely rational agents, each of whom is a **LEGISLATOR** (someone who decides laws) and a **SUBJECT** (someone who has to follow those laws) in what he calls a **KINGDOM OF ENDS**. We can only act on moral laws that would be accepted by this fully rational community - we belong to a moral parliament where we are free participators in the law-making process. This introduces an important **SOCIAL** aspect to Kantian ethics. "Kantian ethics is the ethics of democracy," argues James Rachels.

SUMMUM BONUM

The **SUMMUM BONUM** or "supreme good" is **VIRTUE** (a person of "good will" who follows their duty by applying the Categorical Imperative) combined with **HAPPINESS**. We should not act in order to get happiness (because moral action should only involve doing our duty for duty's sake), but the ideal is that we should be happy to the degree that we **DESERVE** to be happy. This is obviously not something that can be found in this life - we see bad people living happy lives and good people living unhappy lives - therefore the Summum Bonum must be able to be achieved in the **AFTERLIFE**.

THREE POSTULATES

Kant argued there are three necessary postulates (or propositions) for morality:

1. **FREEDOM** (we must be free to make moral decisions).

2. **IMMORTALITY** (there must be an afterlife in order to achieve the summum bonum).

3. **GOD** (necessary to guarantee the moral law and to judge fairly and reward or punish).

Strengths of Kant

- It's **REASONABLE** - pretty much what most people consider morality to be about (such as universalising your behaviour). The various formulations of the Categorical Imperative take the **DIGNITY** and **EQUALITY** of human beings very seriously. The **INNOCENT** are protected by the universal equality given to all human beings.

- It's **ABSOLUTE -** it therefore avoids the problems of predicting the outcome associated with teleological theories. The means justify the ends, not the other way around.

Weaknesses

- It is **INFLEXIBLE** as absolutes have to be applied in all situations irrespective of what we consider to be the wisest choice. For example, Kant considers the case of a crazy axeman who arrives at a house where a friend is hiding and asks "is your friend in there?" because truth-telling is an **ABSOLUTE** we are supposed to say "yes."

- Kant also seems to make a clear distinction between our **EMOTIONS** and the ethical choice done from duty alone - but is it really morally doubtful if I act out of emotion like compassion and not just from **DUTY** alone? Also, what happens when two duties **CONFLICT** (for example, the duty to preserve my friend's life conflicts with my duty to tell the truth - Kant's own example where he insists we tell the truth whatever happens).

- Surely **CONSEQUENCES** do matter? Can we not have a **HIERARCHY OF DUTIES** as WD **ROSS** argues so that preserving life is ranked higher than truth-telling?

Key Quotes - Kant

1. *"It is impossible to conceive of anything in the world good without qualification except the good will." Kant*

2. *"Kant places the stern voice of duty at the heart of the moral life." Robert Arrington*

3. *"The highest created good is a world where rational beings are happy and worthy of happiness." Kant*

4. *"With sufficient ingenuity almost every precept can be consistently universalised." Alasdair MacIntyre*

5. *"There is more to the moral point of view than being willing to universalise one's rules." William Frankena*

Confusions

1. "Duty means blind obedience." This is what Adolf Eichmann implied in his trial in 1962 - but it's not Kant's view of duty which involves reasoning through the **UNIVERSALISABILITY** of your action and treating all human beings with equal respect.

2. "Duty means ignoring emotion." This is a possible reading of Kant, but not the only one. Another reading is to say that Kant saw duty as the primary motive and so long as emotions don't conflict with duty then having moral emotions is fine - just don't base your reason on emotion.

GET MORE HELP

Get more help with deontology by using the links below:

http://i-pu.sh/T5P64P60

Natural Moral Law

A normative **DEONTOLOGICAL** theory coming from a **TELEOLOGICAL** worldview as Aristotle argues that the good is defined by the **RATIONAL ENDS** or **FINAL CAUSES** which people by **NATURE** pursue. "Natural Law is the sharing in the eternal law by intelligent creatures" argues **AQUINAS** and calls these rational ends **OBJECTS OF THE WILL**. Key **ASSUMPTIONS** are that we have a fixed human nature, there is an eternal law in God himself, and the **SYNDERESIS** principle - that we naturally "do good and avoid evil."

KEY TERMS

- **APPARENT GOODS** - Acts done from reason which do not correspond to the natural law.

- **REAL GOODS** - Acts done from human reason which correspond to the natural law.

- **ETERNAL LAW** - The law as conceived by God.

- **DIVINE LAW** - The law revealed to humankind in the Bible.

- **HUMAN LAW** - The laws we establish by human reason as our social laws.

- **NATURAL LAW** - "Right reason in agreement with nature." Cicero

- **PRIMARY PRECEPTS** - Principles known innately which define the rational ends or goods of human existence.

- **SECONDARY PRECEPTS** - Applications of the primary precepts using human reason, which are not absolute.

- **NATURAL RIGHTS** - Rights given to human beings because of their very nature as human.

- **SYNDERSIS** - The assumption that we by nature seek to do good and avoid evil - or have an innate knowledge of first principles (the primary precepts).

Synderesis: 'each precious child, born with the desire to do good, and avoid evil'

AQUINAS' ARGUMENT

AQUINAS sought to reconcile Christian thought with Greek thinking (**ARISTOTLE**'s works) discovered in Islamic libraries at the **FALL OF TOLEDO** (1085), when Christian armies reconquered Spain. He sees goodness in the **DIVINE ESSENCE** (nature of God) which has a purpose - the **ETERNAL LAW** - reflected in our **HUMAN NATURE** and the ends we rationally pursue. A key assumption Aquinas makes is called the **SYNDERESIS** principle, that we naturally "do good and avoid evil" - which is the opposite of the **REFORMATION** assumption that "all have sinned and fall short of God's glory" (Romans 3:23). We are born with good natures, able to reason and so pursue good ends or objects of the will. The **DIVINE LAW** reflects God's eternal law and is revealed in holy **SCRIPTURE** (eg Ten Commandments of Exodus 20). From these observable rational ends we get the **PRIMARY PRECEPTS**.

Primary Precepts

There are five observable "goods" or rational ends we pursue. (Acronym **POWER**).

- **P**reservation of life
- **O**rdered society
- **W**orship of God
- **E**ducation
- **R**eproduction

These reflect the **DIVINE WILL** because God designed us with a rational nature in His image. Notice that **VERITATIS SPLENDOR** (1995 Papal document) has subtly changed these - Worship of God becomes **APPRECIATION OF BEAUTY** (to fit with our agnostic age), and it adds

CONCERN for the **ENVIRONMENT** to reflect the new emphasis on stewardship rather than **DOMINION** (Genesis 1:24 "and let man have dominion over the earth"). This indicates that **NATURAL LAW** is not as **ABSOLUTE** as we sometimes think. The fourth type of law is **HUMAN LAW**. For society to **FLOURISH** (Greek telos of **EUDAIMONIA** sees happiness as personal and social flourishing) we need to bring our law in line with the **ETERNAL LAW** of God, or put another way, make it appropriate for **RATIONAL** human beings to fulfil their Godly destiny - being with God forever and being Christlike.

Secondary Precepts

These are **APPLICATIONS** of the **PRIMARY PRECEPTS** and may change eg as our society changes, science advances our understanding of the Divine Mind, or a situation demands it (eg Thou shalt not kill gets suspended in times of war). Aquinas suggests **POLYGAMY** (many wives) may sometimes be justified. We don't necessarily have to accept **ROMAN CATHOLIC** applications eg Abortion is tantamount to murder; Euthanasia breaks the **SANCTITY OF LIFE**; Contraception goes against the natural purpose of sex, which is **REPRODUCTION**, and homosexual behaviour is **INTRINSICALLY DISORDERED** (the phrase used in **HUMANAE VITAE**, 1967). There is another assumption here that there is **ONE HUMAN NATURE** - heterosexual-and so there can't be a gay nature. Modern Psychology (eg **JUNG**) suggests we have male and female aspects to our natures and **CHINESE** philosophy has always talked in terms of **YING** and **YANG** - the two aspects of our nature.

Apparent Goods

We cannot consciously sin because our nature is such that we believe we are "doing good and avoiding evil" - the **SYNDERESIS PRINCIPLE** - even when practising genocide. However, though we rationalise it, this clearly breaks the **ETERNAL LAW** reflected in the **NATURAL LAW** that most rational humans want to **PRESERVE LIFE** (primary precept **P** of **POWER** acronym above). We cannot flourish if we break the Natural Law - in this sense we are being sub-human and irrational (even though we believe otherwise). **AQUINAS** calls these **APPARENT GOODS** - which we mistakenly believe (eg Hitler's genocide) are **REAL GOODS**. We can sin, but not consciously, which is why **EVANGELICALS** dislike Natural law theory - arguing it is unrealistic (our very **REASON** is distorted by sin) and unbiblical (it seems to deny Paul's teaching on **ORIGINAL SIN**, inherited from **ADAM** after the **FALL**).

Strengths

- **AUTONOMOUS AND RATIONAL:** Natural law is an autonomous, rational theory and it is wrong to say that you have to believe in God to make sense of it. Aquinas speaks of "the pattern of life lived according to reason." You could be a Darwinian atheist and believe in natural law derived by empirical observation, with the primary precept of survival (Aquinas' preservation of life). Richard **DAWKINS** (The Selfish Gene) goes so far as to argue for a natural genetic tendency to be altruistic: a lust to be nice. "The theory of Natural Law suggests..morality is **AUTONOMOUS**. It has its own questions, its own methods of answering them, and its own standards of truth, and religious considerations are not the point." Rachels (2006:56)

- **AN EXALTED VIEW OF HUMAN BEINGS:** We use reason to work out how to live. So we are not slaves to our passions or our genes. Natural Law has a purpose: a flourishing society and a person fulfilled and happy - **EUDAIMONIA**. It is not ultimately about restricting us by rules, but setting us free to fulfil our proper purpose or **TELOS**, inherent in our design: to rationally assent to personal growth. If we can agree on our purpose we can agree on what morality is for. Moreover, we don't have to accept the fact/value division inherent in Moore or Ayer's philosophy. "The natural world is not to be regarded merely as a realm of facts, devoid of value or purpose. Instead, the world is conceived to be a **RATIONAL ORDER** with value and purpose built into its very nature." Rachels (2006: 50)

- **FLEXIBLE:** Natural Law is not inflexible. The primary precepts may be general and unchanging, but as Aquinas argued, **SECONDARY PRECEPTS** can change depending on circumstances, culture and worldview. The Doctrine of **DOUBLE EFFECT** is also a way to escape the moral dilemmas which exist when two rules conflict, (See Louis Pojman 2006: 47-51) - so not as **ABSOLUTE** as textbooks suggest.

Weaknesses

- **A FIXED HUMAN NATURE:** Aquinas believes in one fixed, shared human nature with certain natural properties eg heterosexual. But evidence suggests there are gay genes and so there is no one natural human nature, but many. This is actually a form of the **NATURALISTIC FALLACY**, the movement from an "is" to an "ought." "It may be that sex does produce babies, but it does not follow that sex ought or ought not to be engaged in only for that purpose. Facts are one thing, values are another." Rachels (2006:52)

- **AN OPTIMISTIC VIEW:** Aquinas believes that we possess **INNATELY** (are born with) a "tendency to do good and avoid evil," the **SYNDERESIS** principle. This is in contrast with Augustine who believes that, due to the Fall, we are born into sin, the sin of Adam, or perhaps the view of psychologists like Freud, that natural selfishness becomes moralised by upbringing and socialisation.

- **IMMORAL OUTCOMES:** Natural Law has been interpreted to ban contraception, because this interferes with the natural primary precept of reproduction. But:

   a.   it's not clear that sex is exclusively for reproduction, in fact, the function of human bonding may be primary;

   b.   the consequence of this policy in Africa has had evil effects of the spread of **HIV/AIDS** and the birth of **HIV** infected children who often become orphans living on the streets.

Key Quotes - Natural Law

1. *"The Natural Law is the sharing in the eternal law by intelligent creatures."* Thomas Aquinas

2. *"Our ultimate end is unrelated good, namely God, who alone can fill our will to the brim because of infinite goodness."* Thomas Aquinas

3. *"The Natural Law is unchangeable in its first principles, but in its secondary principles it may be changed through some special causes hindering the following of the primary precepts."* Thomas Aquinas

4. *"The Natural Law involves universality as it is inscribed in the rational nature of a person; it makes itself felt in every person endowed with reason."* Veritatis Splendor (1995)

5. *"There exist acts which are always seriously wrong by reason of their object."* Veritatis Splendor (1995)

6. *"Every marital act must of necessity retain its intrinsic relationship to the procreation of human life."* Humanae Vitae (1967)

7. *"The theory of Natural Law suggests morality is autonomous. It has its own questions, its own methods of answering them and its own standards of truth. Religious considerations are not the point."* James Rachels

8. *"The world is conceived as a rational order with value and purpose built into its very nature."* James Rachels

Confusions

1. "Natural" means "as we see in the natural world." This isn't true because many things we see in the natural world we would argue are immoral (eg killing the weak which animals do all the time). "Natural" means something closer to "appropriate for our rational human nature," for example, we may naturally feel lust but it is irrational and wrong to seek to indulge this lust with a complete stranger.

2. "Natural law is dogmatic and inflexible." This is a wrong reading of Aquinas who himself argues that the **SECONDARY PRECEPTS** are liable to change with circumstances and our developed understanding. It is quite possible to be a natural law theorist and argue in favour of contraception on the grounds that it is necessary to save lives and reduce population growth.

GET MORE HELP

Get more help with natural law by using the links below:

http://i-pu.sh/T7F79V41

Virtue Ethics

Virtue ethics is the ethics of **CHARACTER**. What habits of character do I need to develop to build a good life? Its origins lie in Greek and Roman philosophy - **ARISTOTLE'S** Nichomachean Ethics (his lecture notes taken by his son Nichomachus - fourth century BC) is particularly important. His works were preserved by Islam and discovered by Christians at the reconquest of **TOLEDO** in 1085.

AQUINAS (1227-74) then brought together Christian and Aristotelean insights in his **SUMMA THEOLOGICA. NATURAL LAW** and **VIRTUE ETHICS** should really be taught together: They are complementary, and share a common telos of **EUDAIMONIA** (flourishing or well-being). Aquinas adds **THEOLOGICAL VIRTUES** (faith, hope and love as in 1 Corinthians 13) to more traditional ones (like the Greek virtues of courage, wisdom, temperance and fortitude).

KEY TERMS

- **ARETE** - Greek for virtue (skill, excellence are alternative words for virtue).

- **EUDAIMONIA** - the Greek word for flourishing or self-realisation (sometimes translated happiness).

- **GOLDEN MEAN** - Aristotle's idea of a judgement point between two vices, the vice of deficiency and the vice of excess, achieved by practical wisdom.

- **PHRONESIS** - the Greek moral virtue of practical wisdom or prudence.

- **SOPHIA** - the Greek word for intellectual wisdom.

- **TEMPERANCE** - a key Greek virtue meaning moderation.

FOUR CRITICISMS OF ACTION-BASED ETHICS

Action-based ethics cannot answer the question "why should I be moral?" Deontological ethics (eg **KANT**) focuses on negatives, on "thou shalt nots" looking primarily at the **INDIVIDUAL** but providing inadequate **MOTIVATION** to follow the rules laid down.

Action-based ethics are based on an outdated **THEOLOGICAL-LEGAL MODEL** of ethics. **NATURAL LAW** is based on **DIVINE LAW** coming from God where God is the **SOVEREIGN** ruler. **KANTIAN** ethics also focuses on rigid a priori **RULES**, with justice ultimately in the hands of **GOD** in the afterlife (the postulate of immortality).

Action-based theories ignore the spiritual dimension of ethics. Humans need to realise **POTENTIAL** and aspire to a range of emotional and spiritual goals, such as **INTEGRITY** and internal **PEACE**.

Action-based theories neglect the **COMMUNAL** basis of ethics. MacIntyre argues that Enlightenment philosophers like **KANT** overplay **AUTONOMY**. Ethics is rooted in community and shared practices and values. Virtues like **SYMPATHY**, kindness and friendship need strong communities to be expressed.

TELEOLOGICAL WORLDVIEW

The Greek worldview is **TELEOLOGICAL**. Everything has a true purpose (telos) sometimes called the **FINAL CAUSE**. For example, the final cause (or aim or object) of good eating is health - the efficient cause (realising that aim) a nicely balanced diet. Louis Pojman explains it this way:

> *"Humanity has an essence or a function. Just as it is a function of a doctor to cure the sick, and the function of a knife to cut well, so it is the function of humans to use reason in pursuit of the good life (eudaimonia). The virtues indicate the kind of political-moral characteristics necessary for people to attain happiness." Pojman (2006:161)*

The final end of human life is to **FLOURISH (EUDAIMONIA** sometimes translated happiness but very different to Bentham's hedonic view). To flourish we need to build **MORAL** virtue through the practice of **PHRONESIS** (prudence, judgement, practical wisdom) and **INTELLECTUAL** virtue (eg **TECHNE** or technical wisdom eg being good at **ICT**).

The goal is **EXCELLENCE** or good **SKILL**. So the Greek word for virtue (**ARETE**) means excellence, skill or habit. Rooney is an excellent (aretaic) footballer and Nelson Mandela an excellent (aretaic) person.

TWO WORDS FOR WISDOM (SOPHIA AND PHRONESIS)

It's important to understand the two different words for wisdom in Greek, relating to the **CONTEMPLATIVE** and the **CALCULATIVE** mental processes.

INTELLECTUAL skills build **SOPHIA** - we can become a very wise scientist or literary critic. But the good **MORAL** character is built by (rather than builds - note the difference) **PHRONESIS** (the calculative intellectual skill of practical wisdom or right judgement).

So ...

SKILL (PHRONESIS) + KNOWLEDGE (eg of IDEAL VIRTUES) = the GOOD LIFE (FLOURISHING)

There are three ways of gaining phronesis (three Es):

- **EMULATE** your heroes (so heroism is important)

- **EDUCATE** yourself (teachers are important)

- **EXPERIENCE** life (think about your mistakes and learn from them)

No wonder Greeks respected the old and in Sparta the rule was by a small group of **PHRONIMOI** (wise men) - one of their jobs was to decide whether babies lived or were "exposed" on a hillside (male) or thrown off a cliff "female" because they were thought to be **WEAK**.

The virtuous character is built by **PHRONESIS**, the moral/intellectual virtue of practical wisdom - the skill of making decisions in difficult or different circumstances. Whereas **SOPHIA** is the end result of practising the intellectual virtues (such as **TECHNE**), phronesis is gained by exercising right moral judgement.

You can gain three As at A level - **SOPHIA** - but still act like a fool - lacking **PHRONESIS**. The excellent life requires both measures of wisdom.

VIRTUE AS HABIT

Virtues need to be practised as habits until they become instincts, combining **REASON** and **EMOTION**. Over time we build a good character as a tree puts down roots and produces good fruit - and will need a good gardener (teacher) and soil (environment) to flourish (**EUDAIMONIA**).

This process needs **DISCIPLINE** - and it will be important to have good role models who show the virtues of **TEMPERANCE** and **FORTITUDE**. Rooney may be a skilful (**ARETE** - virtue or skill) footballer but he's a bad role model when he swears to the camera after scoring a hat-trick.

Part of postmodern confusion is that our **HEROES** are not good characters - so how are we to flourish if we follow **THEM**? Greek heroes had **FLAWS** - deliberately so (Achilles was jealous and childish), that's so we learn from their **VICES** as well.

GOLDEN MEAN

The **GOLDEN MEAN** is not a midpoint, but a judgement point somewhere between two vices, the **VICE OF DEFICIENCY** (lack of virtue) and the **VICE OF EXCESS** (too much virtue) which depends on the **SITUATION**.

That's why we need to develop the skill/virtue of **PHRONESIS** (right judgement). "Be angry for the right reason, with the right person, for the right length of time" said **ARISTOTLE** (how often the person getting mad is not really mad at you).

So the **VICE OF DEFICIENCY** is indifference (we should be very angry at genocide) and the **VICE OF EXCESS** is violent temper (anger can be inappropriate and we "lose it"). **PHRONESIS** makes the **APPROPRIATE** decision as we become wise and flourish, building **HABITS** that fulfil our potential (personal potential and also for society generally).

GOLDEN MEANIE

ABSOLUTE OR RELATIVE

The list for virtues changes according to our **CULTURE** and time. So Spartans share with us a love of courage, but don't share with us their practice of killing the weaker babies, **INFANTICIDE**. They also practised slavery, were very liberated in some ways in their attitudes to women (who could own property) and believed you needed to kill a Macedonian to prove you were strong enough to be a warrior.

ARISTOTLE'S list of virtues includes some familiar ones (courage, justice, temperance) and but also unexpected ones such as **MAGNIFICENCE** (close to the Christian vice of **PRIDE** meaning roughly buy the best not the cheapest). **AQUINAS** adds the **THEOLOGICAL** virtues of faith (faithfulness, trust), hope (persevering belief) and love (the Greek **AGAPE** or sacrificial, commitment love even for the stranger).

So virtues seem to be **RELATIVE** - but is there some **UNIVERSAL** virtue (friendship? courage? sympathy?) - which might indicate an element of **ABSOLUTE** morality as well?

MACINTYRE AFTER VIRTUE

Moral philosophy entered a dead end argues **MACINTYRE** when it lost sight of the **TELOS** of human action - the goal of **FLOURISHING** a naturalistic feature because it depends on human nature and **GOODS INTERNAL TO PRACTICES**. Morality makes sense within the roles we play in our own forms of life, with agreed, shared aims rules and obligations (family life, village life, company life, school life). When we know the **TELOS** (goal, purpose) of our form of life we will know what habits of character to develop to reinforce and strengthen it.

If we cannot agree on the **TELOS** (aim) then we cannot decide whether **KANT'S** ethics is better than **MILL'S**. The **ENLIGHTENMENT** shifted the emphasis from character to action. Then in the 20TH century **META-ETHICS** and the influence of **LOGICAL POSITIVISM/EMOTIVISM** of AJ **AYER** and others (Moore, Hare) began to dominate and questions of **MEANING** became the central focus of ethics (not "Am I a good person?" but "What does good mean?").

The **NATURALISTIC FALLACY** was accepted as valid, whereas **MACINTYRE** argues agreement about a **TELOS** is an Aristotelean way of escaping the is/ought problem (where the goal or telos is eudaimonia - personal and social flourishing).

Modern naturalists like MacIntyre argue that as long as we can agree on the meaning of **EUDAIMONIA** (even if the view may change over time as psychology gives us new insight into the human condition), then we can escape the naturalistic fallacy. What is more, we can begin to answer the question posed by Socrates, but then abandoned by **EMOTIVISM**: "How then should we live?"

Strengths

- **HOLISTIC** view of human nature. Reason is applied through **PHRONESIS** or practical wisdom, but unlike Kant, the emotions are not ignored, as virtue ethics is holistic (includes emotion in the building of character). To Aristotle personal and social flourishing (**EUDAIMONIA**) is the final rational goal, and reason tames and moralises the desires and appetites of the irrational part of our soul.

- **CHARACTER-BASED** - Habits of character are central, developed through **TRAINING** ... we need heroes who are moral role models as well as virtuous (= skilful) footballers. The present age is "instrumental" in the sense of things being a means to an end, and **PRAGMATIC**, in that we tend to "bend the rules." Behind action lies character: it may be legal for an **MP** to claim expenses for a duck house, but is it honest?

- **PARTIALITY** - Both Kant and Mill require impartiality for their ethical viewpoints, for example, Mill says: "Utilitarianism requires the moral agent to be strictly impartial, as a disinterested and benevolent spectator." James **RACHELS** comments: "It may be doubted whether impartiality is really such an important feature of the moral life ... some virtues are partial and some are not. Love and friendship involve partiality towards loved ones and friends; beneficence (doing good) towards people in general is also a virtue ... what is needed is not some general requirement of impartiality, but an understanding of how the different virtues relate to each other" (2007:173-4).

Weaknesses

- **RELATIVISTIC** - We cannot agree what the key virtues are, which differ from culture to culture eg Al Qaeda thinks it is virtuous to be a suicide bomber. One person's terrorist is another person's freedom fighter and hero, so goodness must depend on something else. Perhaps we can escape this problem (as **MACINTYRE** argues we can) by defining what, for me or for my society, are the virtues which will make me (or us) **FLOURISH**.

- "Aristotle saw pride as a special virtue, Christians see it as a master vice." Rachels (2007:166)

- **DECISIONS** are difficult. "It is not obvious how we should go about deciding what to do" Rachels (2007:176) **ANSCOMBE** argues we should get rid of the idea of "right action" altogether and just use virtue words eg "unjust," "dishonest." William **FRANKENA** has argued "virtues without principles are blind," and virtues don't tell us where we get our principles. **RACHELS** argues that virtue ethics is incomplete because it can't account for the fact that "being honest" implies a rule, so "it's hard to see what honesty consists in if it is not the disposition to follow such rules." Rachels (2007:177).

- **CONFLICTING VIRTUES** - What happens when virtues conflict, for example, when honesty and kindness conflict, or honesty and loyalty to one's friends? "It only leaves you wondering which virtue takes precedence," concludes Rachels. Louis **POJMAN** comments: "Virtue ethics has the problem of application: it doesn't tell us what to do in particular instances in which we most need direction." (2006:166)

Confusions

The **GOLDEN MEAN** means moderation. This isn't the case. Aristotle makes clear that it may be appropriate to show extreme anger in circumstances (think of cruelty or genocide for example). The mean is a judgement point which can only be fixed by the **CIRCUMSTANCES**. It isn't a balance point.

Virtue ethics cannot handle moral decision-making. This argument is hotly disputed. Elizabeth **ANSCOMBE** argued that consequentialism couldn't handle decisions because of the impossibility of knowing the consequences, and deontology had lost its way in rules and regulations and "thou shalt nots." Virtue ethics, in stressing the learnt skill or right judgment, was the most practical way of reaching decisions as it retains a **FLEXIBILITY**. Fairness, for example, depends on a consideration of all relevant facts, not the application of a rule.

KEY QUOTES

1. *"The soul of the students must be conditioned by good habits just as land must be cultivated to nurture seed."* Aristotle

2. *"We need to attend to virtues in the first place in order to understand the function and authority of rules."* Alasdair MacIntyre

3. *"Morality is internal and has to be expressed as 'be this' not 'do this'."* Leslie Stephens

4. *"We may even go as far as to say that the person who doesn't enjoy doing noble actions isn't a good person at all."* Aristotle

5. *"Virtue ethics is an ethics of aspiration, not an ethics of duty."* Richard Taylor

6. *"The mean and the best course is the course of virtue."* Aristotle

7. *"There must first be a disposition to excellence - to love what is fine and loathe what is base."* Aristotle

GET MORE HELP

Get more help with virtue ethics by using the links below:

http://i-pu.sh/S6Z07B10

Meta-Ethics

META-ETHICS means "beyond ethics" (metaphysics - beyond physics). Rather than asking how we derive moral principles like "do not kill," meta-ethics asks us to consider what moral statements mean. Here are some of the key issues:

Is there an **OBJECTIVE** principle we can appeal to resolve moral disputes? Or are we inevitably in a world of **RELATIVISM** and **SUBJECTIVISM** where such questions are "up to me?"

When I say "stealing is wrong" am I describing some **FACTS** about the world which we can look at, examine, appeal to, or am I only stating an opinion or expressing a feeling?

Is moral **LANGUAGE** a special type of language where words like "good" and "ought" mean something quite specific and different from other uses of, for example, "good?" Is the meaning of good in the sentence "that's a good painting" different from the moral use "good boy!?"

KEY TERMS

- **ANALYTIC** - True by definition "all bachelors are unmarried."

- **A POSTERIORI** - After experience.

- **A PRIORI** - Before experience.

- **COGNITIVISM** - Moral facts can be known objectively.

- **NATURALISM** - Moral goodness is a feature of the natural world, and so an a posteriori fact.

- **NATURALISTIC FALLACY** - You cannot move without supplying a missing **PREMISE** from a descriptive statement such as "kindness causes pleasure" to a moral statement: "kindness is good."

- **SYNTHETIC** - True by observation: "John is a bachelor."

Note: Hume was himself a naturalist arguing that morality derives from the natural feeling of sympathy. He never said: "You cannot move from an ought to an is," but only that if we do so, we must provide a missing premise with a value-statement in it, such as "pleasure is good as it leads to a happy life."

COGNITIVE OR NON-COGNITIVE

COGNITIVISTS believe goodness can be known as an **OBJECTIVE** feature of the world - where "objective" means "out there where it can be analysed, measured, and assessed."

Something about our reason allows us to do this either by making some measurement (for example, of happiness as the utilitarians do) or working out a principle **A PRIORI** (before experience) as Kant argues we do in deriving the **CATEGORICAL IMPERATIVE**.

NON-COGNITIVISTS argue there is no objective, factual basis for morality - it is subjective and up to me to determine.

The **NATURALISTS** argue we can resolve this issue empirically (**A POSTERIORI** - from experience) by looking at some observable feature of an action - a fact such as "it causes pain" (a utilitarian concern) or "it fulfils the natural rational purpose of human beings" (the **EUDAIMONIA** or goal of flourishing of virtue ethics).

NON-NATURALISTS argue either that the truth is a priori (Kant for example) or that there are simply no facts which we can identify as moral facts - so that making a moral statement adds nothing to what we already know from a factual basis. This form of non-naturalism is called **EMOTIVISM**.

THE NATURALISTIC FALLACY

Starting with David Hume philosophers like GE **MOORE** have argued that when we move from a description about the real world to a moral statement we make a leap from a naturalistic statement to a **PRESCRIPTIVE** statement (one with "ought" in it). This prescription is doing something different. What we often fail to do is explain the missing link between a description and a prescription - and this leap from "is" to "ought" is what is known as the naturalistic fallacy. AN Prior (1949) explains the fallacy:

> *"Because some quality or combination of qualities invariably accompanies the quality of goodness, this quality or combination of qualities is identical with goodness. If, for example, it is believed that whatever is pleasant is good, or that whatever is good must be pleasant, or both, it is committing the naturalistic fallacy to infer from this that goodness and pleasantness are the same quality. The naturalistic fallacy is the assumption that because the words 'good' and 'pleasant' necessarily describe the same objects, they must attribute the same quality to them."*

MOORE argued that goodness cannot be a **COMPLEX** analysable property of an action. For example a horse can be broken down into animal, mammal, four legs, hairy tail - a **COMPLEX** idea. Because goodness isn't a complex idea, it must be either a **SIMPLE**, indefinable quality or it doesn't refer to anything at all. Since ethics isn't an **ILLUSION**, goodness must consist in a simple **INDEFINABLE QUALITY**, like the colour yellow.

THE OPEN QUESTION

Moore pointed out that the naturalistic fallacy, of implying that goodness was identical to some specific property such as pleasure, is susceptible to the **OPEN QUESTION** attack. Suppose I say: "This ice cream causes me so much pleasure" and then say: "Ice cream is good!." The open question attack suggests I can always ask the question: "It produces pleasure, but nonetheless, is it morally **GOOD**?"

If I can answer "no" to this point then I have proved that goodness is something independent of pleasure.

MOORE'S INTUITIONISM

Moore was a non-naturalist **COGNITIVIST** because he believed that goodness could not be defined by its natural properties, but that we know what we mean by good by a special intuition or perception (so **COGNITIVIST**, as goodness can be known as a shared experience).

Moore argues goodness is an **INDEFINABLE PROPERTY** of an action just as the colour yellow is a non-definable property of a lemon - we know what it is and that's the end of it. We can try and reduce yellowness to light waves but that doesn't precisely tell us what yellow is - yellow just is yellow, we know this by intuition. Notice this is a version of non-naturalism as goodness cannot be established as a fact of sense experience, but as a **NON-NATURALISTIC** perception.

Evaluation of Intuitionism

Moral intuitions are said to be like the **ANALYTIC** truths of Mathematics. But moral statements are more than just "true by definition."

> "Thus the intuitionists lost the one useful analogy to support the existence of a body of truths known by reason alone." Peter Singer

Intuitionists **CAN'T AGREE** what these moral goods are. So how can they be **SELF-EVIDENT**?

If intuitions are actually **CULTURAL CONSTRUCTS** as Freud suggests, then they cannot be **SELF-EVIDENT**.

Moore is arguing that moral truths are similar to **PLATO'S** ideal forms. John Maynard **KEYNES** once commented that: "Moore could not distinguish love, and beauty and truth from the furniture" so enraptured was he by his idealised world of the forms.

Moore confuses a complex thing (colour) for a simple thing (yellow). Goodness is in fact a **COMPLEX** idea, like **COLOUR** because it includes within it a whole class of principles we might describe as good (like colour includes, red, yellow, green, blue).

Moore has confused a general category (colour, goodness) for a specific quality of that category (yellowness, generosity).

UTILITARIAN NATURALISM

Utilitarians are **NATURALISTS** because they argue that goodness is an observable feature of the natural world - part of our **A POSTERIORI** experience of pleasure and pain. So to work out what is good, we need to project into the future and balance the likely pain and pleasure of our choice. That which maximises happiness and minimises pain is good, and actions that do the opposite are bad.

Utilitarians quite openly commit the **NATURALISTIC FALLACY** arguing that it is obviously good to pursue happiness because that as a matter of fact is the goal that all humans are pursuing. They give a **TELEOLOGICAL** justification for goodness, just as virtue ethicists follow Aristotle in linking goodness to **HUMAN FLOURISHING**.

The philosopher **JOHN SEARLE** gives us another naturalist way out of the supposed fallacy. If I promise to pay you £500 then I am doing two things - I am agreeing to play the promising game which involves **OBLIGATION** to pay your money back, and I am accepting that part of the rules of the game, fixed by society, is that I only can break this promise if a large, overriding reason appears for doing so (for example, the money is stolen from me and I am bankrupt, so can't pay it back).

So the making of a promise is a **FACT** but because of the logical feature of promising - that I agree it creates obligations for me - this allows us to move to a value statement "you ought to keep your promise."

AYER'S EMOTIVISM ("EXPRESSIVISM")

AJ Ayer (1910-1989) formed part of a school of linguistic philosophy called **LOGICAL POSITIVISM** which had at its heart the **VERIFICATION PRINCIPLE**. Truth claims had to be verified true or false by sense-experience. His theory is a theory of **NON-COGNITIVISM** as he argues moral statements add no facts - just opinions which cannot be established true or false empirically. So moral truth cannot be **KNOWN**.

> "The fundamental ethical concepts are unanalysable inasmuch as there is no criterion by which to judge the validity of the judgements. They are mere pseudo-concepts. The presence of an ethical symbol adds nothing to its factual content. Thus if I say to someone 'You acted wrongly in stealing the money,' I am not stating anything more than if I had simply stated 'you stole the money'." Language, Truth and Logic (1971)

This approach to moral language was a development of **HUME'S FORK** - an argument about language developed by David Hume. Hume argued that statements about the real world were of two sorts - they were either analytic or synthetic: either **LOGICAL TRUTHS** or **STATEMENTS OF FACT**.

An analytic statement is true by definition (2+2=4), a synthetic statement true by experience. So "all bachelors are unmarried" is true by definition, whereas "John is a bachelor" is true by experience (John might be married so that would make the statement **EMPIRICALLY** false). As moral statements are neither analytic (they'd have nothing useful to say about the **REAL** world if they were) or synthetic (not **VERIFIABLE**) they are logically and empirically meaningless.

Ayer put the same point another way.

> *"The presence of an ethical symbol in a proposition adds nothing to its factual content." (1971:142)*

Ayer believed that problems arose when the **NATURALISTS**, such as the **UTILITARIANS** claimed an empirical basis for goodness in the balance of pleasure over pain. What happens when one person's pleasure is another person's pain? Consider that someone steals your wallet. To you, stealing is wrong because it causes you pain. To the thief, stealing is good, because it gives her money to buy food, and she's starving. Stealing appears to be **BOTH** right and wrong at the same time.

This contradictory result indicates there can be no **FACT** of morality - just an **OPINION**.

> *"It is not self-contradictory to say some pleasant things are not good, or that some bad things are desired." (1971:139)*

Ayer means by this that if I say, "You were wrong to steal" there is no additional **FACT** introduced by the word "wrong" - only an **EXPRESSION** of a feeling of disapproval. Note he argues the word **GOOD** is not describing a feeling but, in is own words "**EVINCING**" a feeling - like letting out a squeal if you hit your thumb.

> *"Stealing money is wrong expresses no proposition which can be either true or false. It's as if I had written "stealing money!!!" where the exclamation marks show a special sort of moral disapproval." AJ Ayer*

Evaluation of Ayer

Ayer's view seems to be a radical **SUBJECTIVISM** suggesting morality is just "up to me." It is a form of **RELATIVISM** that makes moral debate impossible.

Ayer's view is based on a **FALLACY**. Ludwig Wittgenstein demonstrated that language is part of a game we play with shared rules. **MORAL** language is neither analytic nor synthetic but rather, **PRESCRIPTIVE**. Ayer has committed a fallacy like saying, "The world is either square or flat." It's neither.

According to Alasdair MacIntyre in After Virtue, emotivism obliterates the distinction between manipulative and non-manipulative behaviour. There is no longer such an idea as a **VALID REASON**. Moral discourse is simply about manipulating you to my point of view.

MORAL PROGRESS

CL STEVENSON'S EMOTIVISM (INTEREST THEORY)

Stevenson argued that three criteria must be fulfilled when we use the word "good":

1. We must be able to agree that the action is good;

2. The action must have a **MAGNETISM** - we must want to do it, and feel an **INTEREST** in its being done;

3. The action cannot be verified empirically by appeal to facts.

So moral language has an **EMOTIVE** meaning and a **PERSUASIVE** meaning - we are encouraging others to share our attitude. This is why we bother to **ARGUE** about ethics, whereas on questions of taste we "agree to differ."

> "Good has an emotive meaning ... when a person morally approves of something, he experiences a rich feeling of security when it prospers and is indignant or shocked when it doesn't."
> CL Stevenson.

RM HARE'S PRESCRIPTIVISM

RM Hare (1919-2002) argued that moral judgements have an **EMOTIVE** and a **PRESCRIPTIVE** meaning.

Prescriptions are forms of **IMPERATIVE**: "you oughtn't steal" is equivalent to saying, "**DON'T STEAL!**."

Hare agrees that you cannot derive a **PRESCRIPTION** such as "Run!"

from a description, "there's a bull over there!" as there is a **SUBJECTIVE** element (I may choose to walk calmly or stand and wave my red rag). I am free to judge, hence the title of his book **FREEDOM** and **REASON**.

Hare follows **KANT** (even though Hare is a preference utilitarian) in arguing that **REASONABLENESS** lies in the **UNIVERSALISABILITY** of moral statements. Anyone who uses terms like "right" and "ought" are **LOGICALLY COMMITTED** to the idea that any action in relevantly similar circumstances is also wrong (see Kant's first formula of the **CATEGORICAL IMPERATIVE**).

So if Nazis say, "Jews must be killed," they must also judge that if, say it turns out that they are of Jewish origin then they too must be killed. Only a **FANATIC** would say this.

Hare argues for the importance of **MORAL PRINCIPLES** rather than **RULES**. It is like learning to drive a car:

> *"The good driver is one whose actions are so exactly governed by principles which have become a habit with him, that he normally does not have to think what to do. But all road conditions are various, and therefore it is unwise to let all one's driving become a matter of habit." (Language of Morals p 63)*

Evaluation of Prescriptivism

Hare is still denying there are **OBJECTIVE** moral truths. We are free to choose our own principles and determine our actions according to our desires and preferences - there is no objective right and wrong independent of our choosing, but then having chosen, we must be able to universalise it. As a **NON-NATURALIST** he avoids reference to any final **TELOS** such as human flourishing.

Philippa **FOOT** criticised Hare in her lecture in 1958 ("Moral Beliefs") for allowing terribly immoral acts (and people) to be called "moral" simply because they are **CONSISTENT**. We cannot avoid approving the statement: "If I was a Jew, I would want to be dead too." Prescriptivism cannot help justifying **FANATICISM**.

In his later book **MORAL THINKING** Hare brings together **PRESCRIPTIVISM** and his version of **PREFERENCE UTILITARIANISM**. To prescribe a moral action is to universalise that action - in universalising, "I must take into account all the ideals and preferences held by all those who will be affected and I cannot give any weight to my own ideals. The ultimate effect of this application of universalisability is that a moral judgement must ultimately be based on the maximum possible satisfaction of the preferences of all those affected by it."

Hare's pupil **PETER SINGER** builds on this idea to give prescriptivism an **OBJECTIVE** basis in his own version of preference utilitarianism. We are asked to universalise from a neutral, universal viewpoint.

So in the end prescriptivism escapes the charge of being another form of radical subjectivism.

THE LEGACY OF DAVID HUME

David Hume argued that morality was a matter of acting on desires and feelings. Moral reasoning really reduces to the question: "What do I want?" - it remains radically **SUBJECTIVE**. If Hume is right, there is no answer to the question: "Why should I be moral?" or "Why should I be benevolent?." If I don't want to be moral, that seems to be the end of the argument.

JL **MACKIE** (Inventing Right and Wrong,1977) argues that the common view of moral language implies that there are some objective moral facts in the universe. But this view is a **MISTAKE**. There are no moral facts. We can only base our moral judgements on **FEELINGS** and **DESIRES**.

The **INTUITIONISTS** (GE Moore, HA Prichard, WD Ross) are arguing that there are **MORAL FACTS** but that we can only know them **NON-NATURALLY** as internal intuitions. This seems to be an attempt to have our cake and eat it.

RM **HARE** does have an answer to the question: "Why should I be moral?." At least in his later book **MORAL THINKING** Hare argues that people are more likely to be happy if they follow universal **PRESCRIPTIVISM** and reason from a viewpoint that takes into account the interests and preferences of all people affected by my decision. However, this is an appeal to **SELF-INTEREST** - Hare is still an **SUBJECTIVIST**.

Following **ANSCOMBE's** essay in 1958 the revival of Virtue ethics suggest a **NATURALIST** reason for being moral: we are moral to achieve personal and social **FLOURISHING**. If we can share the insights of psychology and philosophy we can come to a shared (if still **RELATIVISTIC**, cultural) view of what will build the excellent life.

Naturalism has undergone a resurgence in the twentieth century, led by Geoffrey **WARNOCK** (1971, The Object of Morality) and Alasdair **MACINTYRE** (1981, After Virtue).

More recent, subtler attempts to escape **SUBJECTIVISM** are to be found in John **RAWLS'** A Theory of Justice, which asks us to assume the role of an avatar in a space ship, imagining we are in an **ORIGINAL POSITION** heading to a new world where we don't know our gender, intelligence, race, or circumstances. What rules would we formulate for this world? Rawls, like Hare, brings **KANT** back into the forefront of meta-ethical debate.

KEY QUOTES

1. *"That which is meant by "good" is the only simple object of thought which is peculiar to ethics." GE Moore*

2. *"As this ought expresses some new relation it is necessary that it should be observed and explained and at the same time that a reason be given." David Hume*

3. *"The use of "That is bad!" implies an appeal to an objective and impersonal standard in a way in which "I disapprove of this; do so as well!" does not. If emotivism is true, moral language is seriously misleading." Alasdair MacIntyre*

4. *"Good serves only as an emotive sign expressing our attitude to something, and perhaps evoking similar attitudes in other persons." AJ Ayer*

5. *"To ask whether I ought to do A in these circumstances is to ask whether or not I will that doing A in these circumstances should become a universal law." RM Hare*

6. *"We have an idea of good ends that morality serves. Even if we are deontologists, we still think that there is a point to morality, and that point has to do with better outcomes - truth-telling generally produces better outcomes than lying. These ends can be put into non-moral language in terms of happiness, flourishing, welfare, or equality."* Louis Pojman

GET MORE HELP

Get more help with **Meta-Ethics** by using the links below:

http://i-pu.sh/J9G14Z51

Justice, Law & Punishment

In this section you should consider theories and scholarship within the three areas, as well as the ways in which they interact, for example, you may explore the link between justice and punishment.

THEORIES OF JUSTICE

PLATO'S Republic sets out his ideas about what justice is in the form of a contrast between a prevailing point of view, and his own. His character, Thrasymachus takes the former perspective, arguing that self-interest and domination of the weakest by the strongest is the obvious basis for a just society. This is challenged by a second character, Glaucon, who advocates social rules as a way of protecting the weak from suffering at the hands of the majority. If all elements of society work together, rather like the human body, there will be **HARMONY**. This can only come about if the desires of each individual are governed by **REASON**, which is interpreted most effectively by the philosophers and rulers, who are best-placed to decide what is best for society as a whole.

Critique of Plato

Plato's ideas in Republic were extremely progressive, concerned as they are with **EQUALITY**. Yet in confining the role of judging to the philosophers and rulers of the day, could his theory be accused of **ELITISM**? Democracy today is concerned with every social group having a say.

"Social Contract" Theories of Justice

HOBBES in Leviathan (published 1651) argued for a contract between the people and their ruler in which the people give up autonomy and agree to accept the leader's authority on issues of rights, laws and in dealing with disputes. For this to be effective and for society to be peaceful, he argued, the ruler should have absolute power and not be subject to the law.

Yet **LOCKE** (Treatise on Civil Government, 1690) argued for a less extreme version of the social contract, tempering the surrender of rights of the people and giving the ruler some subjectivity to the law. The institutions of the state, as shaped by the will of the people, should consider themselves duty-bound to protect the rights and freedoms of individuals under their leadership. These may include freedom of speech, the right to hold property and inheritance laws. The foundations for modern democracy were under construction ...

ROUSSEAU, writing in 1762, moved the social contract to within touching distance of modern democracy, by arguing for an emphasis on people and rulers working together. He could foresee problems with civil government in terms of introducing or formalising inequalities, such as property rights. For civil justice to work, it must be authorised by the general will, which should preserve natural instincts of self-preservation and the alleviation of suffering.

Critique of Social Contract Theories

JS **Mill** in On Liberty (1859) expressed concern with the social contract approach as he foresaw that individuals or minorities might be oppressed by the view of the majority, as codified by law. To combat this danger, he advocated freedom of speech as a less dangerous course than giving an authority the right to gag anyone, be their view wrong or unusual. It may be worth considering this view in light of the 2006 UK Incitement to Racial Hatred Law: Should freedom of speech be absolute? The effectiveness of Social Contract theories can perhaps best be seen in the longevity of the American Declaration of Independence (1776), which is based on the work of Thomas **PAINE**, who argued for all people to be given the right to life, liberty and the pursuit of human happiness.

Connections with Ethical Approaches

These theories can be connected with a **RELATIVE** approach to ethics, as democracy ensures that the rights and freedoms being protected reflect the values held by that particular culture. For example, in Aristotle's day, the rulers could be expected to uphold the rights of slave-owners to control slaves, and husbands, their wives, but this would not be satisfactory in today's Western thinking. However, there have been instances where democratic countries have been criticised for not protecting groups in other countries from oppression by leaders or tribes, for example, in the Rwandan genocide of 1994. Could this suggest that there are **ABSOLUTE** laws of morality that should be universally upheld from culture to culture?

LAW

There is a strong relationship between justice and the law. In a civilised society there should be the expectation that the law will reflect justice, and that justice will be upheld and enforced by the law. Those institutions responsible concerned with the law - notably the government, the courts and the police force are there to keep the peace and punish law-breaking.

Should people always obey the law?

AQUINAS believed there are no absolute duties to obey the law because the law is an arbitrary standard as devised by the state. Only laws that reflect justice carry a moral obligation to be obeyed. This may be used to justify the work of charities such as Hart International, who defy laws governing the crossing of borders in order to bring aid and encouragement to persecuted Christians around the world. It also tallies with his virtue ethics, in upholding justice as above the law.

Critique of Aquinas

Yet it may be asked how, without a certain degree of reverence for, and faith in, the law, society can function without anarchy. If everyone deems themselves capable of sitting in judgement over the law, then how can the law hold any real authority? However, Aquinas did suggest that the law should protect people from causing harm to themselves, and thus he saw it as having a degree of authority over the individual.

JS Mill (1806-1873)

In contrast, Mill argued for a rather minimalistic role for the law, in summarising it as a means of protecting one individual from causing harm to another against their will. He did not consider a role of government to protect people from themselves. In today's terms, the "nanny state" would describe such a role, where the government interfere with the freedom of individuals to decide how to live their lives.

Critique of Mill

Yet to what extent can we assess whether a person's private choices affect another's happiness (to put our discussion in utilitarian terms)? A person may believe they have the right to smoke in their own home, but smoking was estimated to cost the NHS in the UK £5.2 billion in 2005/6 which, it may be argued, could be used to save lives elsewhere in the system.

PUNISHMENT

It is generally believed that for **JUSTICE** to be upheld, and the **LAW** to be respected, there must be accountability for actions, with wrong actions punished in proportion to the transgression.

The Aims of Punishment

David Races Past Village Rivers is an acronym that might help you to remember the five aims of punishment:

1. Deterrence
2. Retribution
3. Protection
4. Vindication
5. Reform

DETERRENCE means to inflict a penalty which acts as a buffer holding back a previous offender or another potential offender from committing a crime. It can be clearly linked with **UTILITARIANISM**, because it can justify why an especially heavy punishment might be given to an offender with the intention of deterring many others with similar ideas, thus alleviating even greater suffering for a larger number. Consider, for example, the fact that Guy Fawkes was hung, drawn and quartered … a gruesome punishment designed to deter any other potential parliament bombers!

RETRIBUTION is the proportional suffering of the offender, for the seriousness of the crime committed. This can be linked with the "eye for an eye, tooth for a tooth" approach in Judaeo-Christian ethics. The aim of this command given to Moses was actually to limit suffering, so that a disproportionate amount of revenge was not taken out on the offender.

This approach can be linked with **VIRTUE ETHICS** - for human beings to flourish, retributive justice must be sought as an obvious moral good.

PROTECTION from the offender can be achieved by incarcerating a person considered dangerous to society. This can clearly be linked with **UTILITARIANISM**, as can the next aim: **VINDICATION** is the recognition that, for the law to be respected, there must be penalties imposed for breaking it. In each of these objectives, the good of society is considered as able to outweigh the pain of the offender.

REFORM is where the offender is punished so as to change their character, and quash their desire to re-offend. One method that is widely used today is restorative justice, where the offender and the victims meet together to discuss their lives and the consequences of the crime. It has led to a number of criminals experiencing remorse, and changing their ways which can only be good for society. Often connected with a Christian approach that puts emphasis on forgiveness and redemption, this aim can be linked with the Truth and Reconciliation Committee of South Africa. Yet some Christian thinkers such as CS **LEWIS**, feared the consequences of taking punishment away from the proportionality inherent in a system based on dessert. Victims might not feel that the punishment is strong enough, or in contrast, professional "reformers" may be given carte blanche to do whatever they think best in order to rehabilitate the criminal. This could include psychological treatments that are controversial or even harmful.

Can capital punishment be justified?

Some argue that for the aims of deterrence and retribution, the death penalty is a necessity for specific crimes such as pre-meditated murder or homicide. Some Christians draw on the eye for an eye principle to justify the death penalty in retribution for the taking of life. Yet others draw on the sanctity of life principle to argue against it. This approach may also be linked with **KANT'S DEONTOLOGY**, which sees certain things as absolute rights and wrongs. **UTILITARIANS** may argue that the sorrow caused by the destruction of one life is far outweighed by the advantages to society of the offender's death; relief for the victim's family, deterrence to others to commit similar crimes, and the cost to society of long-term incarceration.

In Dead Man Walking (1993), Sister Helen Prejean argues that **CAPITAL PUNISHMENT** can never achieve **JUSTICE** because those convicted, held and killed on death row largely resemble the poorest ethnic minorities of the US, a situation of grave inequality.

GET MORE HELP

Get more help with justice, law & punishment by using the links below:

http://i-pu.sh/C6F92R92

Exam Rescue Remedy

1. Build your own scaffolding which represents the logic of the theory. Use a mind map or a summary sheet.

2. Do an analysis of past questions by theme as well as by year. Try writing your own Philosophy of Religion paper based on what hasn't come up recently.

3. Examine examiners' reports for clues as to how to answer a question well.

4. Use the **AREA** approach suggested in this revision guide. **ARGUMENT**- Have I explained the argument (from Plato or Kant for example)? **RESPONSE** - Have I outlined and explained a good range of responses to the argument? **EVALUATION** - Now I have clearly set out positions, what do I think of these? Is mine **A PHILOSOPHICAL** argument and why? Does the original argument stand or fall against the criticisms raised? Why or why not?

5. List relevant technical vocabulary for inclusion in essay (eg efficient cause, form of the good, analytic, synthetic).

6. Prepare key quotes from selected key authors, original/contemporary. Learn some.

7. Contrast and then evaluate different views/theories/authors as some questions ask "which approach is best?" So contrast every approach with one other and decide beforehand what you think.

8. Practise writing for 35 minutes. Don't use a computer, unless you do so in the exam.

9. Always answer and discuss the exact question in front of you, never learn a "model answer." Use your own examples (newspapers, films, documentaries, real life). Be prepared to think creatively and adapt your knowledge to the question.

10. Conclude with your view, justify it (give reasons) especially with "discuss."

Lightning Source UK Ltd.
Milton Keynes UK
UKOW04f2001280314

229041UK00006B/6/P